KT-225-497

ESSENTIAL

Baking

Contents

Introduction

Baking is a wonderfully fulfilling and satisfying past-time. Even the Egyptians enjoyed it, as the paintings of bakers at work indicate on the frescoes of ancient Egyptian tombs. During that period baker's mainly produced unleavened girdle cakes, however bread, which was leavened with brewer's yeast, was made especially for the upper classes.

Today the variety of techniques and recipes available are vast. Yet baking is still an admired profession; with many shops, bakeries and supermarkets selling fresh quality goods. Home-baking however, is equally if not more delicious while being simple and satisfying too. Throughout the generations it has been a family favourite as recipes have been passed from parent to child.

Soft, crumbly, melt-in-the mouth pastry is the result that everyone hopes to achieve when baking. If making shortcrust pastry you will achieve much better results if you take a little care. All that is required is that you treat the pastry delicately and with a light touch. In some recipes 'fresh ready-made shortcrust pastry (pie dough)' and 'fresh ready-made puff pastry (pie dough)' have been suggested. The quality of these supermarket products is extremely high and helps save time for those with a busy lifestyle.

Regardless of which pastry (dough) you choose, it is imperative to pre-heat your oven and bake at the recommended temperature. Before starting to bake you should read the recipe thoroughly. In fact reading it over a couple of times helps you become more familiar with the procedures if you are a beginner. Check the list of ingredients and make sure that you have purchased everything that you need. There is nothing worse than realising half way through making your dish that you have forgotten to buy a vital ingredient. Also, be very accurate when measuring. It is best to have everything pre-measured and stored in separate dishes before you start. This makes baking much easier as everything is at your fingertips.

Another important factor when baking is to ensure that the ingredients are stored at the correct temperature. If you follow these instructions the ingredients will be easier to incorporate and therefore you will achieve a better texture. If you mix cold and warm ingredients together your baking will not be as successful. Therefore, try to avoid mixing ingredients such as cold eggs and butter to warm ingredients as it will change the structure of your mixture.

In this book you will find recreated recipes of well-loved traditional baking dishes combined with modern recipes which experiment with contemporary ingredients. You can choose from breads, cakes, tarts, pies and pastries, which are delicious served on their own or as an after dinner treat. No matter which recipes you choose from in this book your home-baked dishes will be sure to impress your guests.

Eve's Pudding

Serves 6

INGREDIENTS

450 g/1 lb cooking apples, peeled, cored and sliced
75 g/2¾ oz/⅓ cup granulated sugar
1 tbsp lemon juice
50 g/1¾ oz/⅓ cup sultanas (golden raisins)
75 g/2¾ oz/⅓ cup butter
75 g/2¾ oz/⅓ cup caster (superfine) sugar
1 egg, beaten
150 g/5½ oz/1¼ cups self-raising flour
3 tbsp milk
25 g/1 oz/¼ cup flaked (slivered) almonds
custard or double (heavy) cream, to serve

1 Grease an 850 ml/1½ pint/3½ cup ovenproof dish.

2 Mix the apples with the sugar, lemon juice and sultanas (golden raisins). Spoon the mixture into the greased dish.

3 Cream the butter and caster (superfine) sugar together until pale. Gradually add the egg.

4 Carefully fold in the self-raising flour and stir in the milk to give a soft, dropping consistency.

5 Spread the mixture over the apples and sprinkle with the flaked (slivered) almonds.

6 Bake in a preheated oven, 180°C/350°F/Gas Mark 4, for 40-45 minutes until the sponge is golden brown.

7 Serve the pudding hot, with custard or double (heavy) cream.

COOK'S TIP

To increase the almond flavour of this pudding, add 25 g/1 oz/¼ cup ground almonds with the flour in step 4.

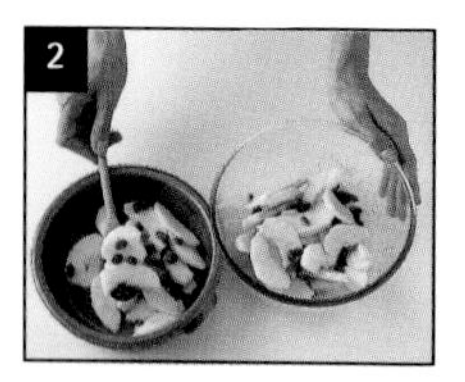

Plum Cobbler

Serves 6

INGREDIENTS

1 kg/2¼ lb plums, stones removed and sliced
100 g/3½ oz /⅓ cup caster (superfine) sugar
1 tbsp lemon juice
250 g/9 oz/2¼ cups plain (all-purpose) flour
75 g/2¾ oz/⅓ cup granulated sugar
2 tsp baking powder
1 egg, beaten
150 ml/¼ pint/⅔ cup buttermilk
75 g/2¾ oz/⅓ cup butter, melted and cooled
double (heavy) cream, to serve

1 Lightly grease a 2 litre/3½ pint/8 cup ovenproof dish.

2 Mix together the plums, caster (superfine) sugar, lemon juice and 25 g/1 oz/¼ cup of the plain (all-purpose) flour.

3 Spoon the mixture into the prepared dish.

4 Combine the remaining flour, granulated sugar and baking powder in a bowl.

5 Add the beaten egg, buttermilk and cooled melted butter. Mix gently to form a soft dough.

6 Place spoonfuls of the dough on top of the fruit mixture until it is almost covered.

7 Bake in a preheated oven, 190°C/375°F/Gas Mark 5, for 35–40 minutes until golden brown.

8 Serve the pudding piping hot, with double (heavy) cream.

COOK'S TIP

If you cannot find buttermilk, try using soured cream.

Raspberry Shortcake

Serves 8

INGREDIENTS

175 g/6 oz/1$^1/_2$ cups self-raising flour
100 g/3$^1/_2$ oz/$^1/_3$ cup butter, cut into cubes
75 g/2$^3/_4$ oz/$^1/_3$ cup caster (superfine) sugar
1 egg yolk
1 tbsp rose water
600 ml/1 pint/2$^1/_2$ cups whipping cream, whipped lightly
225 g/8 oz raspberries, plus a few for decoration

TO DECORATE:
icing (confectioners') sugar
mint leaves

1 Lightly grease 2 baking trays (cookie sheets).

2 To make the shortcakes, sieve (strain) the flour into a bowl.

3 Rub the butter into the flour with your fingers until the mixture resembles breadcrumbs.

4 Stir the sugar, egg yolk and rose water into the mixture and bring together to form a soft dough. Divide the dough in half.

5 Roll each piece of dough to a 20 cm/ 8 inch round and lift each one on to a prepared baking tray (cookie sheet). Crimp the edges of the dough.

6 Bake in a preheated oven, 190°C/375°F/Gas Mark 5, for 15 minutes until lightly golden. Transfer the shortcakes to a wire rack and leave to cool.

7 Mix the cream with the raspberries and spoon on top of one of the shortcakes. Top with the other shortcake round, dust with a little icing (confectioners') sugar and decorate with the extra raspberries and mint leaves.

COOK'S TIP

The shortcake can be made a few days in advance and stored in an airtight container until required.

3

4

5

Chocolate Brownie Roulade

Serves 8

INGREDIENTS

150 g/$5^1/_2$ oz dark chocolate, broken into pieces
3 tbsp water
175 g/6 oz/$^3/_4$ cup caster (superfine) sugar
5 eggs, separated
25 g/1 oz/2 tbsp raisins, chopped
25 g/1 oz pecan nuts, chopped
pinch of salt
300 ml/$^1/_2$ pint/$1^1/_4$ cups double (heavy) cream, whipped lightly
icing (confectioners') sugar, for dusting

1 Grease a 30 × 20 cm/12 × 8 inch swiss roll tin (pan) and line with greased baking parchment.

2 Melt the chocolate with the water in a small saucepan over a low heat until the chocolate has just melted. Leave to cool.

3 Whisk the sugar and egg yolks for 2–3 minutes until thick. Fold in the cooled chocolate, raisins and pecan nuts.

4 Whisk the egg whites with the salt. Fold a quarter of the egg whites into the chocolate mixture, then lightly fold in the rest.

5 Transfer the mixture to the prepared tin (pan) and bake in a preheated oven, 180°C/350°F/Gas Mark 4, for 25 minutes until risen and just firm to the touch. Leave to cool before covering with a sheet of non-stick baking parchment and a damp clean tea towel (dish cloth). Leave to cool completely.

6 Turn the roulade out on to another piece of baking parchment dusted with icing (confectioners') sugar and remove the lining paper.

7 Spread the cream over the roulade. Starting from a short end, roll the sponge away from you using the paper to guide you. Trim the ends of the roulade to make a neat finish and transfer to a serving plate. Leave to chill in the refrigerator until ready to serve. Dust with a little icing (confectioners') sugar before serving, if wished.

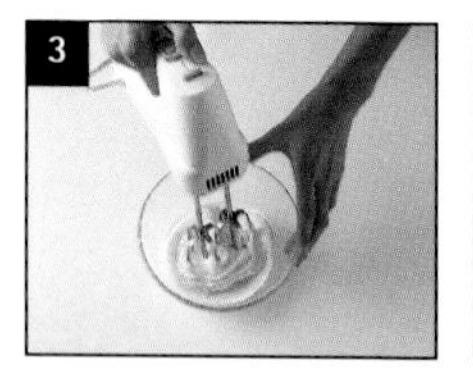
3

3

4

Custard Tart

Serves 8

INGREDIENTS

PASTRY (PIE DOUGH):
150 g/5½ oz plain (all-purpose) flour
25 g/1 oz/5 tsp caster (superfine) sugar
125 g/4½ oz/½ cup butter, cut into small pieces
1 tbsp water

FILLING:
3 eggs
150 ml /¼ pint/⅔ cup single (light) cream
150 ml/¼ pint/⅔ cup milk
freshly grated nutmeg

TO SERVE:
whipping cream

1 To make the pastry (pie dough), place the flour and sugar in a mixing bowl and rub in the butter.

2 Add the water and mix together until a soft pastry (pie dough) has formed. Wrap and leave to chill in the refrigerator for about 30 minutes.

3 Roll out the dough to form a round slightly larger than a 24 cm/ 9½ inch loose-bottomed quiche/flan tin (pan).

4 Line the tin (pan) with the dough, trimming off the edges. Prick the dough with a fork and leave to chill in the refrigerator for 30 minutes.

5 Line the pastry case (pie shell) with foil and baking beans.

6 Bake the tart in a preheated oven, 190°C/375°F/ Gas Mark 5, for 15 minutes. Remove the foil and baking beans and bake the pastry case (pie shell) for a further 15 minutes.

7 To make the filling, whisk together the eggs, cream, milk and nutmeg. Pour the filling into the prepared pastry case (pie shell). Transfer the tart to the oven and cook for 25-30 minutes or until just set. Serve with whipping cream, if wished.

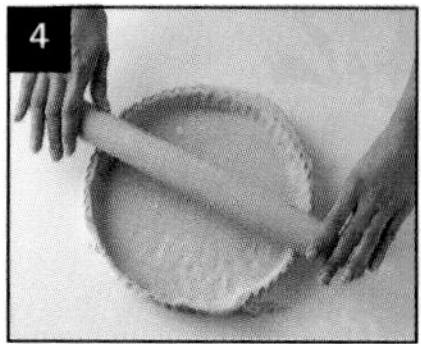

Lemon Tart

Serves 8

INGREDIENTS

PASTRY (PIE DOUGH):
150 g/5½ oz/1¼ cups plain (all-purpose) flour
25 g/1 oz/5 tsp caster (superfine) sugar
125 g/4½ oz/½ cup butter, cut into small pieces
1 tbsp water

FILLING:
150 ml/¼ pint/⅔ cup double (heavy) cream
100 g/3½ oz/½ cup caster (superfine) sugar
4 eggs
grated rind of 3 lemons
12 tbsp lemon juice
icing (confectioners') sugar, for dusting

1 To make the pastry (pie dough), place the flour and sugar in a bowl and rub in the butter. Add the water and mix until a soft pastry (pie dough) has formed. Wrap and leave to chill for 30 minutes.

2 On a lightly floured surface, roll out the dough and line a 24 cm/ 9½ inch loose-bottomed quiche/flan tin (pan). Prick the pastry (pie dough) with a fork and leave to chill for 30 minutes.

3 Line the pastry case (pie shell) with foil and baking beans and bake in a preheated oven, 190°C/ 375°F/ Gas Mark 5, for 15 minutes. Remove the foil and beans and cook for a further 15 minutes.

4 To make the filling, whisk the cream, sugar, eggs, lemon rind and juice together. Place the pastry case (pie shell), still in its tin (pan), on a baking tray (cookie sheet) and pour in the filling.

5 Bake in the oven for about 20 minutes or until just set. Leave to cool, then lightly dust with icing (confectioners') sugar before serving.

1

2

4

Pine Kernel (Nut) Tart

Serves 8

INGREDIENTS

PASTRY (PIE DOUGH):
- 150 g /5 oz/1¼ cups plain (all-purpose) flour
- 25 g/1 oz/5 tsp caster (superfine) sugar
- 125 g/4½ oz/½ cup butter, cut into small pieces
- 1 tbsp water

FILLING:
- 350 g/12 oz curd cheese
- 4 tbsp double (heavy) cream
- 3 eggs
- 125 g/4½ oz/½ cup caster (superfine) sugar
- grated rind of 1 orange
- 100 g/3½ oz pine kernels (nuts)

1 To make the pastry (pie dough), place the flour and sugar in a bowl and rub in the butter with your fingers. Add the water and work the mixture together until a soft pastry (pie dough) has formed. Wrap and leave to chill for 30 minutes.

2 On a lightly floured surface, roll out the dough and line a 24 cm/ 9½ inch loose-bottomed quiche/flan tin (pan). Prick the pastry (pie dough) with a fork and leave to chill for 30 minutes.

3 Line the pastry case (pie shell) with foil and baking beans and bake in a preheated oven, 190°C/ 375°F/ Gas Mark 5, for 15 minutes. Remove the foil and beans and cook the pastry case (pie shell) for a further 15 minutes.

4 To make the filling, beat together the curd cheese, cream, eggs, sugar, orange rind and half of the pine kernels (nuts). Pour the filling into the pastry case (pie shell) and sprinkle over the remaining pine kernels (nuts).

5 Bake in the oven at 170°C/325°F/Gas Mark 3 for 35 minutes or until just set. Leave to cool before serving.

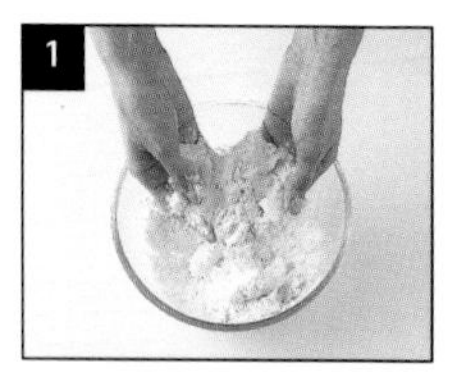
1

2

4

Apricot & Cranberry Frangipane Tart

Serves 8–10

INGREDIENTS

PASTRY (PIE DOUGH):
150 g/5$^1/_2$ oz/1$^1/_4$ cups plain (all-purpose) flour
125 g/4$^1/_2$ oz/$^1/_2$ cup caster (superfine) sugar
125 g/4$^1/_2$ oz/$^1/_2$ cup butter, cut into small pieces
1 tbsp water

FILLING:
200 g/7 oz/1 cup unsalted butter
200g/7 oz/1 cup caster (superfine) sugar
1 egg
2 egg yolks
40 g/1$^1/_2$ oz/6 tbsp plain (all-purpose) flour, sieved (strained)
175 g/6 oz/1$^2/_3$ cups ground almonds
4 tbsp double (heavy) cream
411 g/14$^1/_2$ oz can apricot halves, drained
125 g/4$^1/_2$ oz fresh cranberries

1 Place the flour and sugar in a bowl and rub in the butter. Add the water and work the mixture together until a soft pastry (pie dough) has formed. Wrap and leave to chill for 30 minutes.

2 On a lightly floured surface, roll out the dough and line a 24 cm/9$^1/_2$ inch loose-bottomed quiche/flan tin (pan). Prick the pastry (pie dough) with a fork and chill for 30 minutes.

3 Line the pastry case (pie shell) with foil and baking beans and bake in a preheated oven, 190°C/375°F/Gas Mark 5, for 15 minutes. Remove the foil and beans and cook for a further 10 minutes.

4 Cream together the butter and sugar until fluffy. Beat in the egg and egg yolks, and stir in the flour, almonds and cream.

5 Place the apricots and cranberries in the pastry case (pie shell) and spoon the filling on top.

6 Bake in the oven for about 1 hour, or until the topping is just set. Leave to cool slightly, then serve warm or cold.

Pear Tarts

Makes 6

INGREDIENTS

250 g/9 oz fresh ready-made puff pastry
25 g/1 oz/8 tsp soft brown sugar
25 g/1 oz/6 tsp butter (plus extra for brushing)
1 tbsp stem (candied) ginger, finely chopped
3 pears, peeled, halved and cored
cream, to serve

1 On a lightly floured surface, roll out the pastry (pie dough). Cut out six 10 cm/4 inch rounds.

2 Place the circles on to a large baking tray (cookie sheet) and leave to chill for 30 minutes.

3 Cream together the brown sugar and butter in a small bowl, then stir in the chopped stem (candied) ginger.

4 Prick the pastry circles with a fork and spread a little of the ginger mixture on to each one.

5 Slice the pear halves lengthways, keeping the pears intact at the tip. Fan out the slices slightly.

6 Place a fanned-out pear half on top of each pastry (pie dough) circle. Make small flutes around the edge of the pastry (pie dough) circles and brush each pear half with melted butter.

7 Bake in a preheated oven, 200°C/400°F/Gas Mark 6, for 15–20 minutes until the pastry is well risen and golden. Serve warm with a little cream.

COOK'S TIP

If you prefer, serve these tarts with vanilla ice cream for a delicious dessert.

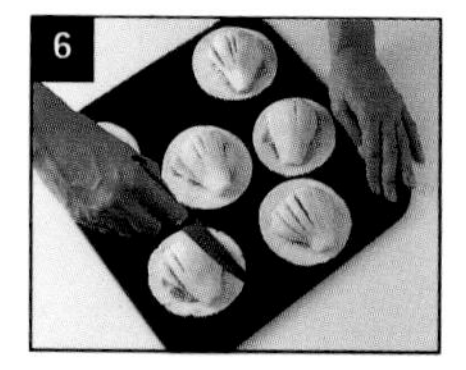

Crème Brûlée Tarts

Makes 6

INGREDIENTS

PASTRY (PIE DOUGH):
150 g/5 oz/1¼ cups plain (all-purpose) flour
25 g/1 oz/5 tsp caster (superfine) sugar
125 g/4½ oz/½ cup butter, cut into small pieces.
1 tbsp water

FILLING:
4 egg yolks
50 g/ 1¾ oz/9 tsp caster (superfine) sugar
400 ml 14 fl oz/1¾ cups double (heavy) cream
1 tsp vanilla flavouring (extract)
demerara (brown crystal) sugar, for sprinkling

1 Place the flour and sugar in a bowl and rub in the butter. Add the water and work the mixture together until a soft pastry (pie dough) forms. Wrap and chill for 30 minutes.

2 Roll out the dough to line six 10 cm/4 inch tart tins (pans). Prick the bottom of the pastry (pie dough) with a fork and leave to chill for 20 minutes

3 Line the pastry cases (pie shells) with foil and baking beans and bake in a preheated oven, 190°C/375°F/Gas Mark 5, for 15 minutes. Remove the foil and beans and cook for 10 minutes until crisp and golden. Leave to cool.

4 Beat the egg yolks and sugar until pale. Heat the cream and vanilla until just below boiling point, then add to the egg mixture, whisking constantly.

5 Place the mixture in a pan and bring to just below the boil, stirring until thick. Do not allow to boil or it will curdle.

6 Leave the mixture to cool slightly, then pour it into the tart tins (pans). Leave to cool and then leave to chill overnight.

7 Sprinkle the tarts with the sugar. Place under a preheated hot grill (broiler) for a few minutes. Leave to cool, then chill for 2 hours before serving.

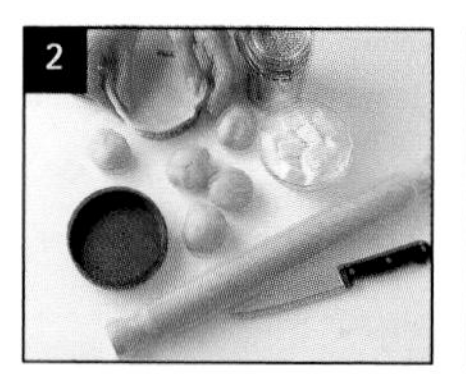

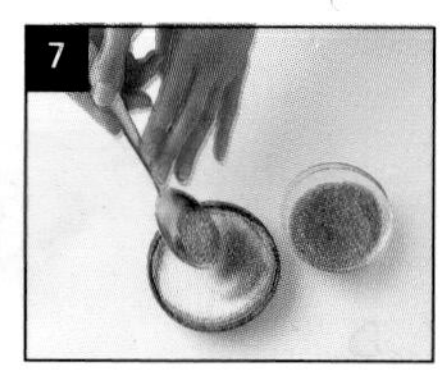

Cinnamon Swirls

Makes 12

INGREDIENTS

225 g/8 oz/2 cups strong white bread flour
1/2 tsp salt
1 sachet easy blend dried yeast
25 g/1 oz/6 tsp butter, cut into small pieces
1 egg, beaten
125 ml/4 fl oz/1/2 cup warm milk
2 tbsp maple syrup

FILLING:
50 g/1 3/4 oz/10 tsp butter, softened
2 tsp ground cinnamon
50 g/1 3/4 oz/3 tbsp soft brown sugar
50 g/1 3/4 oz/1/3 cup currants

1 Grease a 23 cm/9 inch square baking tin (pan).

2 Sieve (strain) the flour and salt into a mixing bowl. Stir in the dried yeast. Rub in the butter with your fingers until the mixture resembles breadcrumbs. Add the egg and milk and mix everything together to form a dough.

3 Place the dough in a greased bowl, cover and leave in a warm place for about 40 minutes or until doubled in size.

4 Knead the dough for 1 minute to knock it back (punch down), then roll out to a rectangle 30 × 23 cm/12 × 9 inches.

5 To make the filling, cream together the butter, cinnamon and brown sugar until light and fluffy. Spread the filling over the dough, leaving a 2.5 cm/1 inch border. Sprinkle over the currants.

6 Roll up the dough like a swiss roll, starting at a long edge, and press down to seal. Cut the roll into 12 slices. Place them in the tin, cover and leave for 30 minutes.

7 Bake in a preheated oven, 190°C/375°F/ Gas Mark 5, for 20–30 minutes or until well risen. Brush with the syrup and leave to cool slightly before serving.

5

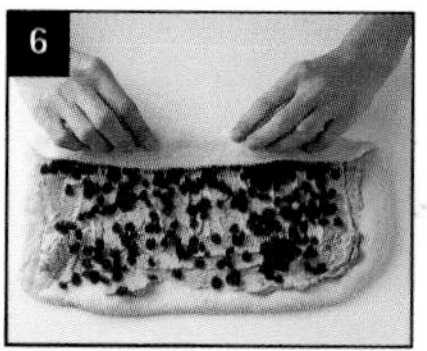
6

6

Orange, Banana & Cranberry Loaf

Serves 8–10

INGREDIENTS

- 175 g/6 oz/1½ cups self-raising flour
- ½ tsp baking powder
- 150 g/5½ oz/1 cup soft brown sugar
- 2 bananas, mashed
- 50 g/1¾ oz chopped mixed peel
- 25 g/1 oz chopped mixed nuts
- 50 g/1¾ oz dried cranberries
- 5-6 tbsp orange juice
- 2 eggs, beaten
- 150 ml/¼ pint/⅔ cup sunflower oil
- 75 g/2¾ oz icing (confectioners') sugar, sieved (strained)
- grated rind of 1 orange

1 Grease a 900 g/2 lb loaf tin (pan) and line the base with baking parchment.

2 Sieve (strain) the flour and baking powder into a mixing bowl. Stir in the sugar, bananas, chopped mixed peel, nuts and cranberries.

3 Stir the orange juice, eggs and oil together until well combined. Add the mixture to the dry ingredients and mix until well blended. Pour the mixture into the prepared tin (pan).

4 Bake in a preheated oven, 180°C/350°F/Gas Mark 4, for about 1 hour until firm to the touch or until a fine skewer inserted into the centre of the loaf comes out clean.

5 Turn out the loaf and leave it to cool on a wire rack.

6 Mix the icing (confectioners') sugar with a little water and drizzle the icing over the loaf. Sprinkle the orange rind over the top. Leave the icing to set before serving the loaf in slices.

COOK'S TIP

This tea bread will keep for a couple of days. Wrap it carefully and store in a cool, dry place.

Crown Loaf

Makes 1 loaf

INGREDIENTS

225 g/8 oz/2 cups strong white bread flour
$^{1}/_{2}$ tsp salt
1 sachet easy blend dried yeast
25 g/1 oz/6 tsp butter, cut into small pieces
125 ml/4 fl oz/$^{1}/_{2}$ cup tepid milk
1 egg, beaten

FILLING:
50 g/1$^{3}/_{4}$ oz/10 tsp butter, softened
50 g/1$^{3}/_{4}$ oz/3 tbsp soft brown sugar
25 g/1 oz chopped hazelnuts
25 g/1 oz stem (candied) ginger, chopped
50 g/1$^{3}/_{4}$ oz mixed (candied) peel
1 tbsp rum or brandy
100 g/3$^{1}/_{2}$ oz/$^{2}/_{3}$ cup icing (confectioners') sugar
2 tbsp lemon juice

1 Grease a baking sheet (cookie sheet). Sieve (strain) the flour and salt into a bowl and stir in the yeast. Rub in the butter. Add the milk and egg and mix together to form a dough.

2 Place the dough in a greased bowl, cover and put in a warm place for 40 minutes until doubled in size. Knead for 1 minute then roll out to a rectangle 30 × 23 cm/12 × 9 inches.

3 Cream together the butter and sugar until light and fluffy. Stir in the hazelnuts, ginger, mixed (candied) peel and rum or brandy. Spread the filling over the dough, leaving a 2.5 cm/1 inch border.

4 Roll up the dough from the long edge to form a sausage shape. Cut into 5 cm/2 inch slices and place on the baking tray (cookie sheet) with the slices just touching. Cover and leave to rise in a warm place for 30 minutes.

5 Bake in a preheated oven, 190°C/325°F/ Gas Mark 5, for 20–30 minutes or until golden. Meanwhile, mix the icing sugar with enough lemon juice to form a thin icing.

6 Leave the loaf to cool slightly before drizzling with icing.

2

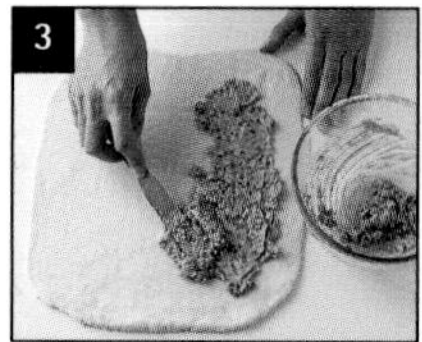
3

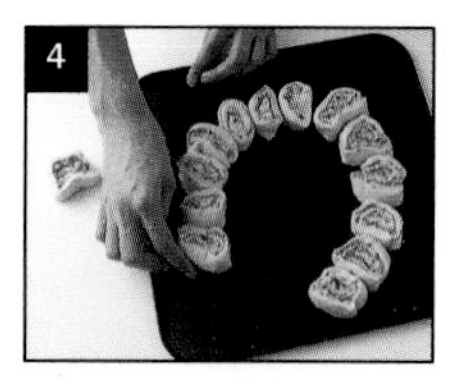
4

Tropical Fruit Bread

Makes 1 loaf

INGREDIENTS

350 g/12 oz/3 cups strong white bread flour
50 g /1¾ oz/5 tbsp bran
½ tsp salt
½ tsp ground ginger
1 sachet easy blend dried yeast
25 g/1 oz/2 tbsp soft brown sugar
25 g/1 oz/6 tsp butter, cut into small pieces
250 ml/9 fl oz/generous 1 cup tepid water
75 g/2¾ oz glacé pineapple, chopped finely
25 g/1 oz dried mango, chopped finely
50 g/1¾ oz /⅔ cup desiccated (shredded) coconut, toasted
1 egg, beaten
2 tbsp coconut shreds

1 Grease a baking sheet (cookie sheet). Sieve (strain) the flour into a large mixing bowl. Stir in the bran, salt, ginger, dried yeast and sugar. Rub in the butter with your fingers, then add the water and mix to form a dough.

2 On a lightly floured surface, knead the dough for about 5–8 minutes or until smooth (alternatively, use an electric mixer with a dough hook). Place the dough in a greased bowl, cover and leave to rise in a warm place until doubled in size.

3 Knead the pineapple, mango and desiccated (shredded) coconut into the dough. Shape into a round and place on the baking tray (cookie sheet). Score the top with the back of a knife. Cover and leave for a further 30 minutes in a warm place.

4 Brush the loaf with the egg and sprinkle with the 2 tbsp coconut. Bake in a preheated oven, 220°C/425°F/Gas Mark 7, for 30 minutes or until golden.

5 Leave the bread to cool on a wire rack before serving.

Soda Bread

Makes 1 loaf

INGREDIENTS

300 g/10½ oz/2½ cups wholemeal (whole wheat) flour
300 g/10½ oz/2½ cups plain (all-purpose) flour
2 tsp baking powder
1 tsp bicarbonate of soda (baking soda)
2 tbsp caster (superfine) sugar
1 tsp salt
1 egg, beaten
425 ml/15 fl oz/1¾ cups natural yogurt

1 Grease and flour a baking tray (cookie sheet).

2 Sieve (strain) the flours, baking powder, bicarbonate of soda (baking soda), sugar and salt into a large bowl.

3 Beat together the egg and yogurt and pour the mixture into the dry ingredients. Combine well to make a soft and sticky dough.

4 On a lightly floured surface, knead the dough for a few minutes until it is smooth, then shape it into a round about 5 cm/2 inches deep.

5 Transfer the dough to the baking tray (cookie sheet). Using a sharp knife, mark a cross shape on the top of the dough.

6 Bake in a preheated oven, 190°C/375°F/ Gas Mark 5, for about 40 minutes or until the bread is golden brown.

7 Transfer the loaf to a wire rack and leave to cool. Cut into slices to serve.

VARIATION

For a fruity version of this soda bread, add 125 g/4½ oz/¾ cup of raisins to the dry ingredients in step 2.

Cheese & Chive Bread

Serves 8

INGREDIENTS

225 g/8 oz/2 cups self-raising flour
1 tsp salt
1 tsp mustard powder
100 g/3½ oz mature (sharp) cheese, grated
2 tbsp chopped fresh chives
1 egg, beaten
25 g/1 oz/6 tsp butter, melted
150 ml/¼ pint/⅔ cup milk

1 Grease a 23 cm/9 inch square cake tin (pan) and line the base with baking parchment.

2 Sieve (strain) the flour, salt and mustard powder into a large mixing bowl.

3 Reserve 3 tbsp of the grated mature (sharp) cheese for sprinkling over the top of the loaf before baking in the oven.

4 Stir the remaining cheese into the bowl along with the chopped fresh chives. Mix well.

5 Add the beaten egg, melted butter and milk and stir the mixture thoroughly.

6 Pour the mixture into the prepared tin (pan) and spread with a knife. Sprinkle over the reserved grated cheese.

7 Bake in a preheated oven, 190°C/375°F/Gas Mark 5, for 30 minutes.

8 Leave the bread to cool slightly in the tin (pan). Turn out on to a wire rack to cool further. Cut into triangles to serve.

COOK'S TIP

You can use any hard mature (sharp) cheese of your choice for this recipe.

4

5

6

Garlic Bread Rolls

Makes 8

INGREDIENTS

12 cloves garlic
350 ml/12 floz/1$^1/_2$ cups milk
450 g/1 lb/4 cups strong white bread flour
1 tsp salt
1 sachet easy blend dried yeast
1 tbsp dried mixed herbs
2 tbsp sunflower oil
1 egg, beaten
milk, for brushing
rock salt, for sprinkling

1 Grease a baking tray (cookie sheet). Peel the garlic cloves and then place them in a pan with the milk, bring to the boil and simmer for 15 minutes. Leave to cool slightly, then process in a blender or food processor to purée the garlic.

2 Sieve (strain) the flour and salt into a large mixing bowl and stir in the dried yeast and mixed herbs.

3 Add the garlic-flavoured milk, sunflower oil and beaten egg to the dry ingredients and mix everything to a dough.

4 Place the dough on a lightly floured work surface and knead lightly for a few minutes until smooth and soft.

5 Place the dough in a greased bowl, cover and leave to rise in a warm place for about 1 hour or until doubled in size.

6 Knock back (punch down) the dough by kneading it for 2 minutes. Shape into 8 rolls and place on the baking tray (cookie sheet). Score the top of each roll with a knife, cover and leave for 15 minutes.

7 Brush the rolls with milk and sprinkle rock salt over the top.

8 Bake in a preheated oven, 220°C/425°F/Gas Mark 7, for 15–20 minutes.

9 Transfer the rolls to a wire rack and leave to cool before serving.

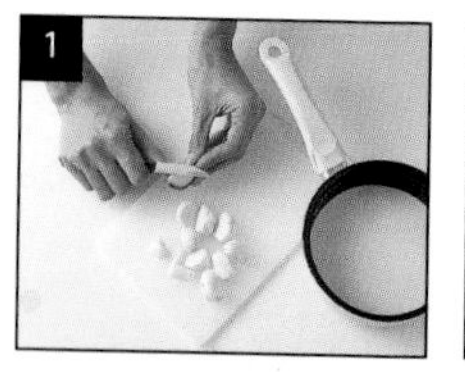
1

3

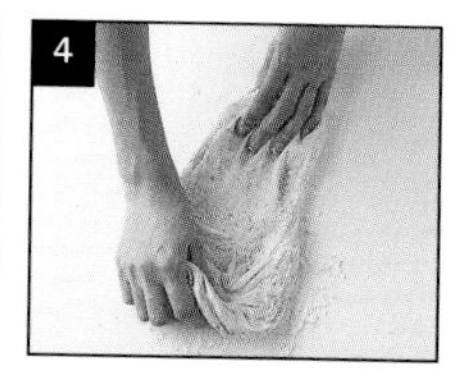
4

Mini Focaccia

Makes 4

INGREDIENTS

350 g/12 oz/3 cups strong white flour
1/2 tsp salt
1 sachet easy blend dried yeast
2 tbsp olive oil
250 ml/9 fl oz tepid water
100 g/3 1/2 oz green or black olives, halved

TOPPING:
2 red onions, sliced
2 tbsp olive oil
1 tsp sea salt
1 tbsp thyme leaves

1 Lightly oil several baking trays (cookie sheets). Sieve (strain) the flour and salt into a large mixing bowl, then stir in the yeast. Pour in the olive oil and tepid water and mix everything together to form a dough.

2 Turn the dough out on to a lightly floured surface and knead it for about 5 minutes (alternatively, use an electric mixer with a dough hook and knead for 7–8 minutes).

3 Place the dough in a greased bowl, cover and leave in a warm place for about 1–1½ hours until it has doubled in size. Knock back (punch down) the dough by kneading it again for 1–2 minutes.

4 Knead half of the olives into the dough. Divide the dough into quarters and then shape the quarters into rounds. Place them on the baking trays (cookie sheets) and push your fingers into the dough to achieve a dimpled effect.

5 Sprinkle the red onions and remaining olives over the rounds. Drizzle the olive oil over the top and sprinkle each round with the sea salt and thyme leaves. Cover and leave the dough to rise again for 30 minutes.

6 Bake in a preheated oven, 190°C/375°F/Gas Mark 5, for 20–25 minutes or until the focaccia are well cooked and golden. Transfer to a wire rack and leave to cool before serving.

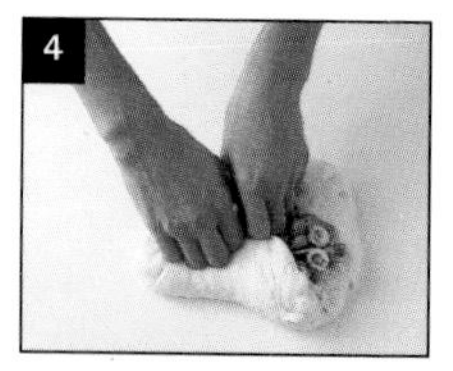

Sun-dried Tomato Rolls

Makes 8

INGREDIENTS

225 g/8 oz/2 cups strong white bread flour
½ tsp salt
1 sachet easy blend dried yeast
100 g/3½ oz/⅓ cup butter, melted and cooled slightly
3 tbsp milk, warmed
2 eggs, beaten
50 g/1¾ oz sun-dried tomatoes, well drained and chopped finely
milk, for brushing

1 Lightly grease a baking tray (cookie sheet).

2 Sieve (strain) the flour and salt into a large mixing bowl. Stir in the yeast, then pour in the butter, milk and eggs. Mix together to form a dough.

3 Turn the dough on to a lightly floured surface and knead for about 5 minutes (alternatively, use an electric mixer with a dough hook).

4 Place the dough in a greased bowl, cover and leave to rise in a warm place for 1–1½ hours until the dough has doubled in size. Knock back (punch down) the dough by kneading it for a few minutes.

5 Knead the sun-dried tomatoes into the dough, sprinkling the work surface (counter) with extra flour as the tomatoes are quite oily.

6 Divide the dough into 8 balls and place them on to the baking tray (cookie sheet). Cover and leave to rise for about 30 minutes until the rolls have doubled in size.

7 Brush the rolls with milk and bake in a preheated oven, 230°C/450°F/Gas Mark 8, for 10–15 minutes until the rolls are golden brown.

8 Transfer the rolls to a wire rack and leave to cool slightly before serving.

3

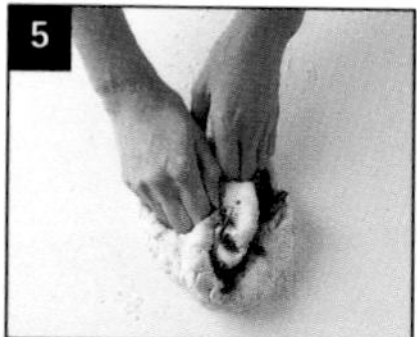

5

6

Puff Potato Pie

Serves 6

INGREDIENTS

750 g/1 lb 9 oz potatoes, peeled and sliced thinly
2 spring onions (scallions), chopped finely
1 red onion, chopped finely
150 ml/$^1/_4$ pint/$^2/_3$ cup double (heavy) cream
500 g/1 lb 2 oz fresh ready-made puff pastry (pie dough)
2 eggs, beaten
salt and pepper

1 Lightly grease a baking tray (cookie sheet). Bring a saucepan of water to the boil, add the sliced potatoes, bring back to the boil and then simmer for a few minutes. Drain the potato slices and leave to cool. Dry off any excess moisture with paper towels.

2 In a bowl, mix together the spring onions (scallions), red onion and the cooled potato slices. Stir in 2 tbsp of the cream and plenty of seasoning.

3 Divide the pastry (pie dough) in half and roll out one piece to a 23 cm/9 inch round. Roll the remaining pastry (pie dough) to a 25 cm/ 10 inch round.

4 Place the smaller circle on to the baking tray (cookie sheet) and top with the potato mixture, leaving a 2.5 cm/1 inch border. Brush this border with a little of the beaten egg.

5 Top with the larger circle of pastry (pie dough), seal well and crimp the edges of the pastry (pie dough). Cut a steam vent in the middle of the pastry (pie dough) and, using the back of a knife, mark with a pattern. Brush with the beaten egg and bake in a preheated oven, 200°C/ 400°F/Gas Mark 6, for 30 minutes.

6 Mix the remaining beaten egg with the rest of the cream and pour into the pie through the steam vent. Return to the oven for 15 minutes, then leave to cool for 30 minutes. Serve warm or cold.

2

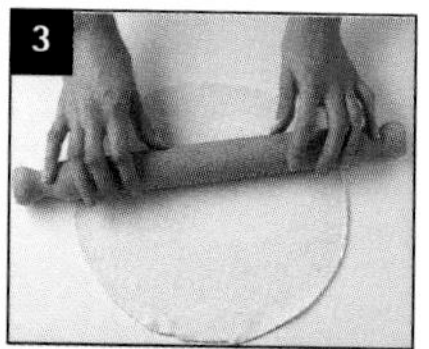
3

4

Provençal Tart

Serves 6–8

INGREDIENTS

250 g/9 oz ready-made fresh puff pastry (pie dough)
3 tbsp olive oil
2 red (bell) peppers, seeded and diced
2 green (bell) peppers, seeded and diced
150 ml/$^{1}/_{4}$ pint/$^{2}/_{3}$ cup double (heavy) cream
1 egg
2 courgettes (zucchini), sliced
salt and pepper

1 Roll out the pastry (pie dough) on a lightly floured surface and line a 20 cm/8 inch loose-bottomed quiche/flan tin (pan). Leave to chill in the refrigerator for 20 minutes.

2 Meanwhile, heat 2 tbsp of the olive oil in a pan and fry the (bell) peppers for about 8 minutes until softened, stirring frequently.

3 Whisk the double (heavy) cream and egg together in a bowl and season to taste with salt and pepper. Stir in the cooked (bell) peppers.

4 Heat the remaining oil in a pan and fry the courgette (zucchini) slices for 4–5 minutes until lightly browned.

5 Pour the egg and (bell) pepper mixture into the pastry case (pie shell).

6 Arrange the courgette (zucchini) slices around the edge of the tart.

7 Bake in a preheated oven, 180°C/350°F/Gas Mark 4, for 35–40 minutes or until just set and golden brown.

COOK'S TIP

This recipe could be used to make 6 individual tarts – use 15 × 10 cm/6 × 4 inch tins (pans) and bake them for 20 minutes.

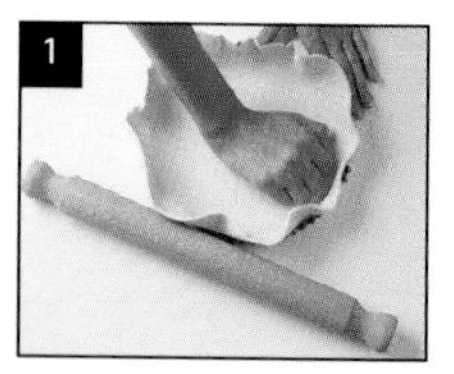

Asparagus & Goat's Cheese Tart

Serves 6

INGREDIENTS

250 g/9 oz fresh ready-made shortcrust pastry (pie dough)
250 g/9 oz asparagus
1 tbsp vegetable oil
1 red onion, chopped finely
200 g/7 oz goat's cheese
25 g/1 oz hazelnuts, chopped
2 eggs, beaten
4 tbsp single (light) cream
salt and pepper

1 On a lightly floured surface, roll out the pastry (pie dough) and line a 24 cm/9½ inch loose-bottomed quiche/flan tin (pan). Prick the base of the pastry (pie dough) with a fork and leave to chill for 30 minutes.

2 Line the pastry case (pie shell) with foil and baking beans and bake in a preheated oven, 190°C/375°F/Gas Mark 7, for about 15 minutes.

3 Remove the foil and baking beans and return the pastry case (pie shell) to the oven for a further 15 minutes.

4 Cook the asparagus in boiling water for 2–3 minutes, drain and cut into bite-size pieces.

5 Heat the oil in a small frying pan (skillet) and fry the onion until soft. Spoon the asparagus, onion and hazelnuts into the prepared pastry case (pie shell).

6 Process the cheese, eggs and cream in a blender until smooth, or beat by hand. Season well, then pour the mixture over the asparagus, onion and hazelnuts.

7 Bake in the oven for 15–20 minutes or until the cheese filling is just set. Serve warm or cold.

VARIATION

Omit the hazelnuts and sprinkle Parmesan cheese over the top of the tart just before cooking in the oven, if you prefer.

2

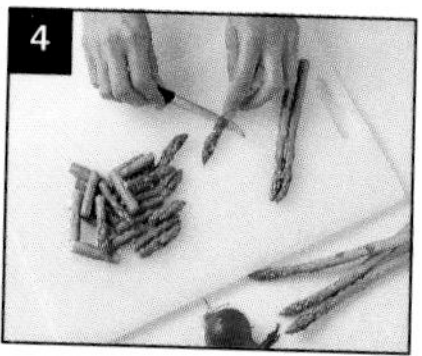
4

6

Mini Cheese & Onion Tarts

Serves 12

INGREDIENTS

PASTRY (PIE DOUGH):
100 g/4$^1/_2$ oz/1 cup plain (all-purpose) flour
$^1/_4$ tsp salt
75 g/2$^3/_4$ oz/$^1/_3$ cup butter, cut into small pieces
1-2 tbsp water

FILLING:
1 egg, beaten
100 ml/3$^1/_2$ fl oz/generous $^1/_3$ cup single (light) cream
50 g/1$^3/_4$ oz Red Leicester cheese, grated
3 spring onions (scallions), chopped finely
salt
cayenne pepper

1 To make the pastry (pie dough), sieve (strain) the flour and salt into a mixing bowl. Rub in the butter with your fingers until the mixture resembles breadcrumbs. Stir in the water and mix to form a dough.

2 Roll out the pastry (pie dough) on to a lightly floured surface. Using a 7.5 cm/3 inch biscuit cutter, stamp out 12 rounds from the pastry (pie dough) and line a patty tin (pan).

3 To make the filling, whisk together the beaten egg, single (light) cream, grated cheese and chopped spring onions (scallions) in a mixing jug (pitcher). Season to taste with salt and cayenne pepper.

4 Pour the filling mixture into the pastry cases (pie shells) and bake in a preheated oven, 180°C/350°F/Gas Mark 4, for about 20–25 minutes or until the filling is just set.

Serve the mini tarts warm or cold.

VARIATION

Top each mini tartlet with slices of fresh tomato before baking, if you prefer.

COOK'S TIP

If you use 175 g/6 oz of ready-made shortcrust pastry (pie dough), these tarts can be made in minutes.

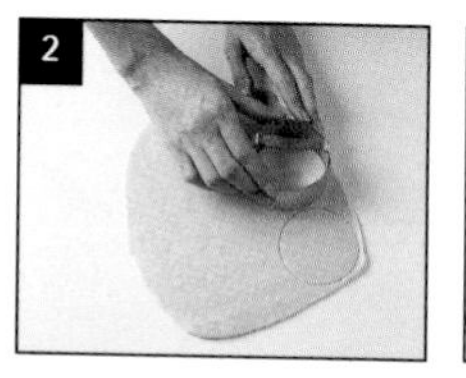

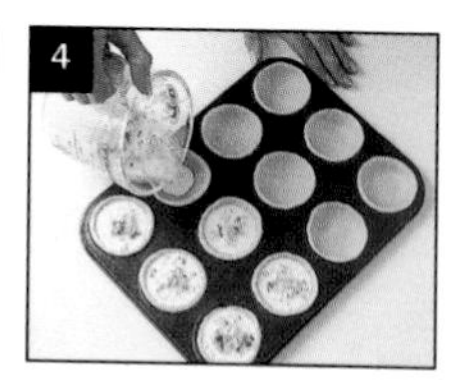

Olive Oil, Fruit & Nut Cake

Serves 8

INGREDIENTS

225 g/8 oz/2 cups self-raising flour
50 g/1¾ oz/9 tsp caster (superfine) sugar
125 ml/4 fl oz/½ cup milk
4 tbsp orange juice
150 ml/¼ pint/⅔ cup olive oil
100 g/3½ oz mixed dried fruit
25 g/1 oz pine kernels (nuts)

1 Grease an 18 cm/7 inch cake tin (pan) and line with baking parchment.

2 Sieve (strain) the flour into a bowl and stir in the caster (superfine) sugar.

3 Make a well in the centre of the dry ingredients and pour in the milk and orange juice. Stir the mixture with a wooden spoon, beating in the flour and sugar.

4 Pour in the olive oil, stirring well so that all of the ingredients are evenly mixed.

5 Stir the mixed dried fruit and pine kernels (nuts) into the mixture and spoon into the prepared tin (pan).

6 Bake in a preheated oven, 180°C/350°F/ Gas Mark 4, for about 45 minutes until the cake is golden and firm to the touch.

7 Leave the cake to cool in the tin (pan) for a few minutes, then transfer to a wire rack to cool.

8 Serve the cake warm or cold and cut into slices.

COOK'S TIP

Pine kernels (nuts) are best known as the flavouring ingredient in the classic Italian pesto, but here they give a delicate, slightly resinous flavour to this cake.

3

4

5

Chocolate & Pear Sponge

Serves 6

INGREDIENTS

- 175 g/6 oz/¾ cup butter, softened
- 175 g/6 oz/1 cup soft brown sugar
- 3 eggs, beaten
- 150 g/5½ oz/1¼ cups self-raising flour
- 15 g/½ oz/2 tbsp cocoa powder
- 2 tbsp milk
- 2 small pears, peeled, cored and sliced

1 Grease a 23 cm/8 inch loose-bottomed cake tin (pan) and line the base with baking parchment.

2 In a bowl, cream together the butter and soft brown sugar until pale and fluffy.

3 Gradually add the beaten eggs to the creamed mixture, beating well after each addition.

4 Sieve (strain) the self-raising flour and cocoa powder into the creamed mixture and fold in gently until all of the ingredients are combined.

5 Stir in the milk, then spoon the mixture into the prepared tin (pan). Level the surface with the back of a spoon or a knife.

6 Arrange the pear slices on top of the cake mixture, arranging them in a radiating pattern.

7 Bake in a preheated oven, 180°C/350°F/Gas Mark 4, for about 1 hour until the cake is just firm to the touch.

8 Leave the cake to cool in the tin (pan), then transfer to a wire rack until completely cold before serving.

COOK'S TIP

Serve the cake with melted chocolate drizzled over the top for a delicious dessert.

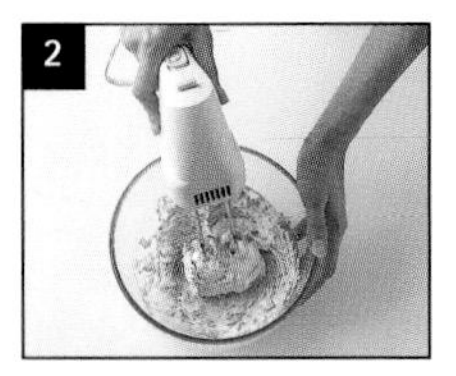

White Chocolate & Apricot Squares

Makes 12 bars

INGREDIENTS

125 g/4½ oz/½ cup butter
175 g/6 oz white chocolate, chopped
4 eggs
125 g/4½ oz/½ cup caster (superfine) sugar
200 g/7 oz/1¾ cups plain (all-purpose) flour, sieved (strained)
1 tsp baking powder
pinch of salt
100 g/3½ oz ready-to-eat dried apricots, chopped

1 Lightly grease a 20 cm/9 inch square cake tin (pan) and line the base with baking parchment.

2 Melt the butter and chocolate in a heatproof bowl set over a saucepan of simmering water. Stir frequently with a wooden spoon until the mixture is smooth and glossy. Remove from the heat and leave the mixture to cool slightly.

3 Beat the eggs and caster (superfine) sugar into the butter and chocolate mixture until well combined.

4 Fold in the flour, baking powder, salt and chopped dried apricots and mix well.

5 Pour the mixture into the tin (pan) and bake in a preheated oven, 180°C/350°F/Gas Mark 4, for 25–30 minutes.

6 The centre of the cake may not be completely firm, but it will set as it cools. Leave in the tin (pan) to cool.

7 When the cake is completely cold turn it out and slice into bars or squares.

VARIATION

Replace the white chocolate with milk or dark chocolate, if you prefer.

2

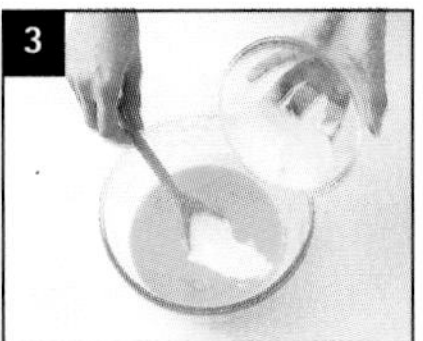
3

4

Crunchy Fruit Cake

Serves 8–10

INGREDIENTS

- 100 g/$3\frac{1}{2}$ oz/$\frac{1}{3}$ cup butter, softened
- 100g/$3\frac{1}{2}$ oz/$\frac{1}{2}$ cup caster (superfine) sugar
- 2 eggs, beaten
- 50 g/$1\frac{3}{4}$ oz/$\frac{1}{3}$ cup self-raising flour, sieved (strained)
- 100 g/$3\frac{1}{2}$ oz/$\frac{2}{3}$ cup polenta (cornmeal)
- 1 tsp baking powder
- 225 g/8 oz mixed dried fruit
- 25 g/ 1oz pine kernels (nuts)
- grated rind of 1 lemon
- 4 tbsp lemon juice
- 2 tbsp milk

1 Grease an 18 cm/7 inch cake tin (pan) and line the base with baking parchment.

2 In a bowl, whisk together the butter and sugar until light and fluffy.

3 Whisk in the beaten eggs a little at a time, whisking well after each addition.

4 Fold the flour, baking powder and polenta (cornmeal) into the mixture until well blended.

5 Stir in the mixed dried fruit, pine kernels (nuts), grated lemon rind, lemon juice and milk.

6 Spoon the mixture into the prepared tin (pan) and level the surface.

7 Bake in a preheated oven, 180°C/350°F/Gas Mark 4, for about 1 hour or until a fine skewer inserted into the centre of the cake comes out clean.

8 Leave the cake to cool in the tin (pan) before turning out.

VARIATION

To give a more crumbly light fruit cake, omit the polenta (cornmeal) and use 150 g/$5\frac{1}{2}$ oz/$1\frac{1}{4}$ cups self-raising flour instead.

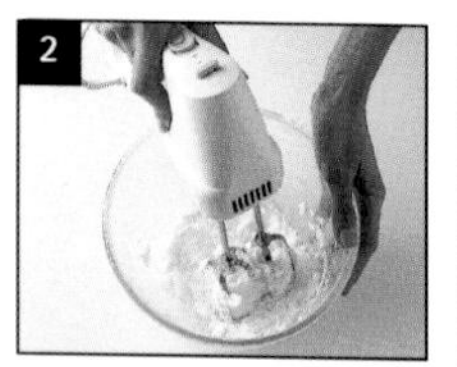
2

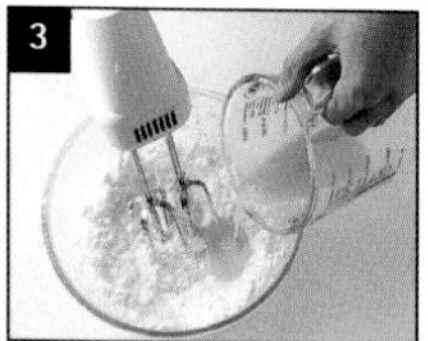
3

5

Carrot Cake

Makes 12 bars

INGREDIENTS

125 g/4 1/2 oz/1 cup self-raising flour
pinch of salt
1 tsp ground cinnamon
125 g/4 1/2 oz/3/4 cup soft brown sugar
2 eggs
100 ml/3 1/2 fl oz/scant 1/2 cup sunflower oil
125 g/4 1/2 oz carrot, peeled and grated finely
25 g/1 oz/1/3 cup desiccated (shredded) coconut
25 g/1 oz/1/3 cup walnuts, chopped
walnut pieces, for decoration

FROSTING:
50 g/1 3/4 oz/10 tsp butter, softened
50 g/1 3/4 oz full fat soft cheese
225 g/8 oz/1 1/2 cups icing (confectioners') sugar, sieved (strained)
1 tsp lemon juice

1 Lightly grease a 20 cm/8 inch square cake tin (pan) and line with baking parchment.

2 Sieve (strain) the flour, salt and ground cinnamon into a large bowl and stir in the brown sugar. Add the eggs and oil to the dry ingredients and mix well.

3 Stir in the grated carrot, desiccated (shredded) coconut and chopped walnuts.

4 Pour the mixture into the prepared tin (pan) and bake in a preheated oven, 180°C/350°F/Gas Mark 4, for 20–25 minutes or until just firm to the touch. Leave to cool in the tin (pan).

5 Meanwhile, make the cheese frosting. In a bowl, beat together the butter, full fat soft cheese, icing (confectioners') sugar and lemon juice until the mixture is fluffy and creamy.

6 Turn the cake out of the tin (pan) and cut into 12 bars or slices. Spread with the frosting and then decorate with walnut pieces.

2

3

5

Apple Cake with Cider

Makes a 20-cm/8-inch cake

INGREDIENTS

- 225 g/8 oz/2 cups self-raising flour
- 1 tsp baking powder
- 75 g/2$^{3}/_{4}$ oz/$^{1}/_{3}$ cup butter, cut into small pieces
- 75 g/2 $^{3}/_{4}$ oz/$^{1}/_{3}$ cup caster (superfine) sugar
- 50 g/1$^{3}/_{4}$ oz dried apple, chopped
- 75 g/2 $^{3}/_{4}$ oz/5 tbsp raisins
- 150 ml/$^{1}/_{4}$ pint/$^{2}/_{3}$ cup sweet cider
- 1 egg, beaten
- 175 g/6 oz raspberries

1 Grease a 20 cm/8 inch cake tin (pan) and line with baking parchment.

2 Sieve (strain) the flour and baking powder into a mixing bowl and rub in the butter with your fingers until the mixture resembles fine breadcrumbs.

3 Stir in the caster (superfine) sugar, chopped dried apple and raisins, and mix well.

4 Pour in the sweet cider and egg and mix together until thoroughly blended. Stir in the raspberries very gently so they do not break up.

5 Pour the mixture into the prepared cake tin (pan).

6 Bake in a preheated oven, 190°C/375°F/ Gas Mark 5, for about 40 minutes until risen and lightly golden. Leave the cake to cool in the tin (pan), then turn out on to a wire rack. Leave until completely cold before serving.

VARIATION

If you don't want to use cider, replace it with clear apple juice, if you prefer.

3

4

4

Apple Shortcakes

Makes 4

INGREDIENTS

150 g/5½ oz/1¼ cups plain (all-purpose) flour
½ tsp salt
1 tsp baking powder
1 tbsp caster (superfine) sugar
25 g/1 oz/6 tsp butter, cut into small pieces
50 ml/2 fl oz/¼ cup milk
icing (confectioners) sugar, for dusting

FILLING:
3 dessert apples, peeled, cored and sliced
100 g/3½ oz/½ cup caster (superfine) sugar
1 tbsp lemon juice
1 tsp ground cinnamon
300 ml/½ pint/1⅓ cups water
150 ml/¼ pint/⅔ cup double (heavy) cream, whipped lightly

1 Lightly grease a baking tray (cookie sheet).

2 Sieve (strain) the flour, salt and baking powder into a bowl. Stir in the sugar, then rub in the butter until the mixture resembles fine breadcrumbs. Pour in the milk and mix everything to a soft dough.

3 Knead the dough, then roll out to a thickness of 1 cm/½ inch. Stamp out 4 rounds, using a 5 cm/2 inch cutter. Transfer the rounds to the prepared baking tray (sheet). Bake in a preheated oven, 220°C/425°F/Gas Mark 7, for about 15 minutes until the shortcakes are well risen and lightly browned. Leave to cool.

4 To make the filling, place the apple slices, sugar, lemon juice and cinnamon in a saucepan. Add the water, bring to the boil and simmer uncovered for 5–10 minutes until the apples are tender. Leave to cool a little, then remove the apples from the pan.

5 To serve, split the shortcakes in half. Place each bottom half on an individual serving plate and spoon on a quarter of the apple slices, then the cream. Place the other half of the shortcake on top. Serve dusted with icing (confectioners') sugar, if wished.

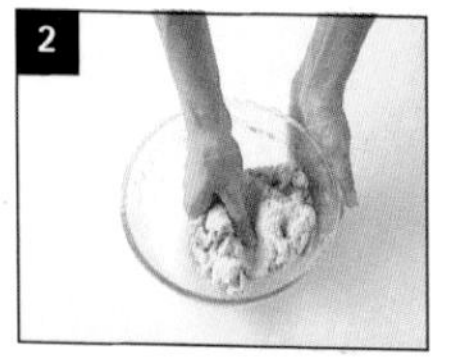
2

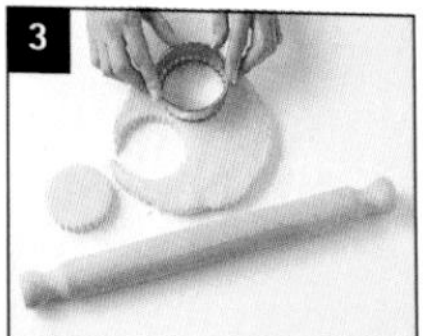
3

4

Cherry Scones

Makes 8

INGREDIENTS

225 g/8 oz/2 cups self-raising flour
1 tbsp caster (superfine) sugar
pinch of salt
75 g/2 3/4 oz/1/3 cup butter, cut into small pieces
40 g/1 1/2 oz/3 tbsp glacé (candied) cherries, chopped
40 g/1 1/2 oz/3 tbsp sultanas (golden raisins)
1 egg, beaten
50 ml/2 fl oz/1/4 cup milk

1 Lightly grease a baking tray (cookie sheet).

2 Sieve (strain) the flour, sugar and salt into a mixing bowl and rub in the butter with your fingers until the scone mixture resembles breadcrumbs.

3 Stir in the glacé (candied) cherries and sultanas (golden raisins). Add the beaten egg.

4 Reserve 1 tablespoon of the milk for glazing, then add the remainder to the mixture. Mix together to form a soft dough.

5 On a floured surface, roll out the dough to a thickness of 2 cm/3/4 inches and cut out 8 scones, using a 5 cm/2 inch cutter.

6 Place the scones on to the baking tray (cookie sheet) and brush with the reserved milk.

7 Bake in a preheated oven, 220°C/425°F/Gas Mark 7, for 8–10 minutes or until the scones are golden brown.

8 Leave to cool on a wire rack, then serve split and buttered.

COOK'S TIP

These scones will freeze very successfully but they are best defrosted and eaten within 1 month.

3

4

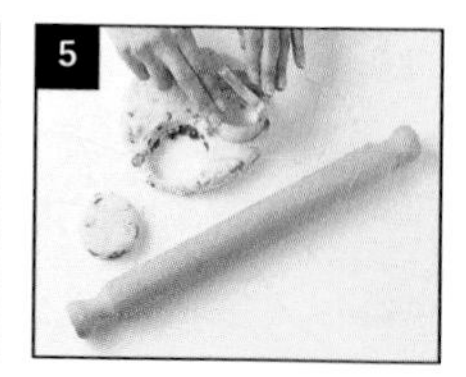

5

Caraway Biscuits (Cookies)

Makes about 36

INGREDIENTS

225 g/8 oz/2 cups plain (all-purpose) flour
pinch of salt
100 g/3½ oz/⅓ cup butter, cut into small pieces
225 g/8 oz/1¼ cups caster (superfine) sugar
1 egg, beaten
2 tbsp caraway seeds
demerara (brown crystal) sugar, for sprinkling (optional)

1 Lightly grease several baking trays (cookie sheets).

2 Sieve (strain) the flour and salt into a mixing bowl. Rub in the butter with your fingers until the mixture resembles fine breadcrumbs. Stir in the caster (superfine) sugar.

3 Reserve 1 tbsp beaten egg for brushing the biscuits (cookies). Add the rest of the egg and the caraway seeds to the mixture and bring together to form a soft dough.

4 On a lightly floured surface, roll out the biscuit (cookie) dough thinly and then cut out about 36 rounds with a 6 cm/2½ inch biscuit (cookie) cutter.

5 Transfer the rounds to the prepared baking trays (cookie sheets), brush with the reserved egg and sprinkle with demerara (brown crystal) sugar.

6 Bake in a preheated oven, 160°C/325°F/Gas 3, for 15 minutes until lightly golden and crisp.

7 Leave the biscuits (cookies) to cool on a wire rack and store in an airtight container.

VARIATION

Caraway seeds have a nutty, delicate anise flavour. If you don't like their flavour, replace the caraway seeds with the milder-flavoured poppy seeds.

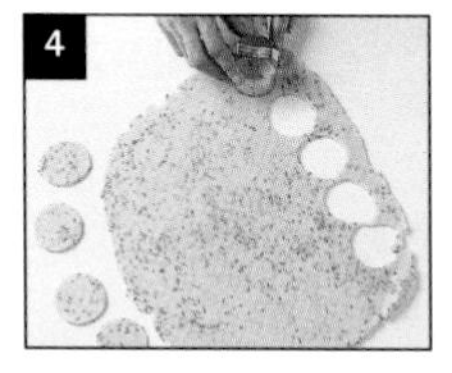

Hazelnut Squares

Makes 16

INGREDIENTS

150 g/5 1/2 oz/1 1/4 cups plain (all-purpose) flour
pinch of salt
1 tsp baking powder
100 g/3 1/2 oz/1/3 cup butter, cut into small pieces
150 g/5 1/2 oz/1 cup soft brown sugar
1 egg, beaten
4 tbsp milk
100 g/3 1/2 oz/1 cup hazelnuts, halved
demerara (brown crystal) sugar, for sprinkling (optional)

1 Grease a 23 cm/9 inch square cake tin (pan) and line the base with baking parchment.

2 Sieve (strain) the flour, salt and baking powder into a large mixing bowl.

3 Rub in the butter with your fingers until the mixture resembles fine breadcrumbs. Stir in the brown sugar.

4 Add the egg, milk and nuts to the mixture and mix well.

5 Spoon the mixture into the prepared cake tin (pan) and level the surface. Sprinkle with demerara (brown crystal) sugar, if using.

6 Bake in a preheated oven, 180°C/350°F/Gas Mark 4, for about 25 minutes or until the mixture is firm to the touch when pressed with a finger.

7 Leave to cool for 10 minutes, then loosen the edges with a round-bladed knife and turn out on to a wire rack. Cut into squares.

VARIATION

For a coffee time biscuit (cookie), replace the milk with the same amount of cold strong black coffee, the stronger the better!

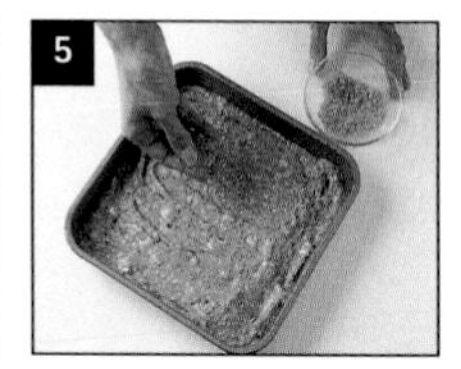

Oat & Raisin Biscuits (Cookies)

Makes 10

INGREDIENTS

50 g/1¾ oz/10 tsp butter
125 g/4½ oz/½ cup caster (superfine) sugar
1 egg, beaten
50 g/1¾ oz/½ cup plain (all-purpose) flour
½ tsp salt
½ tsp baking powder
175 g/6 oz/2 cups porridge oats
125 g/4½ oz/¾ cup raisins
2 tbsp sesame seeds

1 Lightly grease 2 baking trays (cookie sheets).

2 In a large mixing bowl, cream together the butter and sugar until light and fluffy.

3 Add the beaten egg gradually and beat until well combined.

4 Sieve (strain) the flour, salt and baking powder into the creamed mixture. Mix well.

5 Add the porridge oats, raisins and sesame seeds and mix well.

6 Place spoonfuls of the mixture well apart on the prepared baking trays (cookie sheets) and flatten them slightly with the back of a spoon.

7 Bake in a preheated oven, 180°C/350°F/Gas Mark 4, for 15 minutes.

8 Leave the biscuits (cookies) to cool slightly on the baking trays (cookie sheets).

9 Transfer the biscuits (cookies) to a wire rack and leave to cool completely before serving.

VARIATION

Substitute chopped ready-to-eat dried apricots for the raisins, if you prefer.

COOK'S TIP

To enjoy these biscuits (cookies) at their best, store them in an airtight container.

Millionaire's Shortbread

Makes 12 bars

INGREDIENTS

175 g/6 oz/1 1/2 cups plain (all-purpose) flour
125 g/4 1/2 oz/1/2 cup butter, cut into small pieces
50 g/1 3/4 oz/3 tbsp soft brown sugar, sieved (strained)

TOPPING:
50 g/1 3/4 oz/10 tsp butter
50 g/1 3/4 oz/3 tbsp soft brown sugar
400 g/14 oz can condensed milk
150 g/5 1/2 oz milk chocolate

1 Grease a 23 cm/9 inch square cake tin (pan).

2 Sieve (strain) the flour into a mixing bowl and rub in the butter with your fingers until the mixture resembles fine breadcrumbs. Add the sugar and mix to form a firm dough.

3 Press the dough into the prepared tin (pan) and prick with a fork.

4 Bake in a preheated oven, 190°C/375°F/ Gas Mark 5, for 20 minutes until lightly golden. Leave to cool in the tin (pan).

5 To make the topping, place the butter, sugar and condensed milk in a non-stick saucepan and cook over a gentle heat, stirring constantly, until the mixture comes to the boil.

6 Reduce the heat and cook for 4–5 minutes until the caramel is pale golden and thick and is coming away from the sides of the pan. Pour the topping over the shortbread base and leave to cool.

7 When the caramel topping is firm, melt the milk chocolate in a heatproof bowl set over a saucepan of simmering water. Spread the melted chocolate over the topping, leave to set in a cool place, then cut the shortbread into squares or fingers to serve.

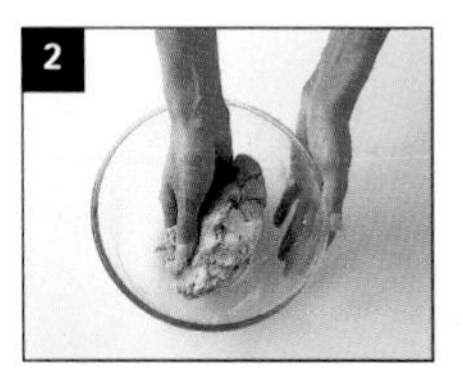

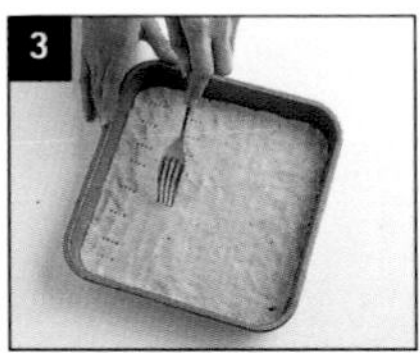

Vanilla Hearts

Makes about 16

INGREDIENTS

225 g/8 oz/2 cups plain (all-purpose) flour
150 g/5$\frac{1}{2}$ oz/$\frac{2}{3}$ cup butter, cut into small pieces
125 g/4$\frac{1}{2}$ oz/$\frac{1}{2}$ cup caster (superfine) sugar
1 tsp vanilla flavouring (extract)
caster (superfine) sugar, for dusting

1 Lightly grease a baking tray (cookie sheet).

2 Sieve (strain) the flour into a large mixing bowl and rub in the butter with your fingers until the mixture resembles fine breadcrumbs.

3 Stir in the caster (superfine) sugar and vanilla flavouring (extract) and bring the mixture together with your hands to make a firm dough.

4 On a lightly floured surface, roll out the dough to a thickness of 2.5 cm/1 inch. Stamp out 12 hearts with a heart-shaped biscuit cutter measuring about 5 cm/2 inches across and 2.5 cm/1 inch deep.

5 Arrange the hearts on the prepared baking tray (cookie sheet). Bake in a preheated oven, 180°C/350°F/Gas Mark 4, for 15–20 minutes until the hearts are a light golden colour.

6 Transfer the vanilla hearts to a wire rack and leave to cool. Dust with a little caster (superfine) sugar just before serving.

COOK'S TIP

Place a fresh vanilla pod in your caster (superfine) sugar and keep it in a storage jar for several weeks to give the sugar a delicious vanilla flavour.

2

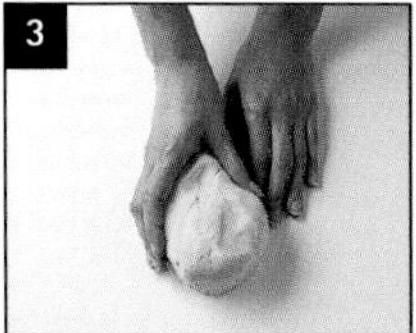

3

4

Rock Drops

Makes 8

INGREDIENTS

200 g/7 oz/1^3/4 cups plain (all-purpose) flour
2 tsp baking powder
100 g/3^1/2 oz/^{1}/3 cup butter, cut into small pieces
75 g/2^3/4 oz/^{1}/3 cup demerara (brown crystal) sugar
100 g/3^1/2 oz/^{1}/2 cup sultanas (golden raisins)
25 g/1 oz/2 tbsp glacé (candied) cherries, chopped finely
1 egg, beaten
2 tbsp milk

1 Lightly grease a baking tray (cookie sheet).

2 Sieve (strain) the flour and baking powder into a mixing bowl. Rub in the butter with your fingers until the mixture resembles breadcrumbs.

3 Stir in the sugar, sultanas (golden raisins) and chopped glacé (candied) cherries.

4 Add the beaten egg and the milk to the mixture and bring together to form a soft dough.

5 Spoon 8 mounds of the mixture on to the baking tray (cookie sheet). Make sure they are spaced well apart as they will spread during cooking.

6 Bake in a preheated oven, 200°C/400°F/Gas Mark 6, for about 15–20 minutes until firm to the touch when pressed with a finger.

7 Remove the rock drops from the baking tray (cookie sheet). Either serve piping hot from the oven or transfer to a wire rack and leave to cool before serving.

COOK'S TIP

For convenience, prepare the dry ingredients in advance and just before cooking stir in the liquid.

2

3

5

This is a Parragon Book
This edition published in 2002
Parragon
Queen Street House
4 Queen Street
Bath BA1 1HE, UK

ISBN: 0-75256-942-2

Copyright © Parragon 2000

All rights reserved. No part of this publication may be reproduced, stored in a retrieval system or transmitted, in any form or by any means, electronic, mechanical, photocopying, recording or otherwise, without the prior permission of the copyright holder.

Printed in China

Note

Cup measurements in this book are for American cups. Tablespoons are assumed to be 15 ml. Unless otherwise stated, milk is assumed to be full fat, eggs are medium and pepper is freshly ground black pepper.